I0554981

THE MIRROR OF ALCHEMY

FR. ROGER BACON, OFM

Professor at the University of Oxford

Dalcassian Publishing Company

PHILADELPHIA, PA

Library of Congress Cataloging-in-Publication Data

CHAPTER I.
Of the Definitions of Alchemy.

In many ancient Books there are found many definitions of this Art, the intentions whereof we must consider in this Chapter. For Hermes said of this Science: Alchemy is a Corporal Science simply composed of one and by one, naturally conjoining things more precious, by knowledge and effect, and converting them by a natural commixtion into a better kind. A certain other said: Alchemy is a Science, teaching how to transform any kind of metal into another: and that by a proper medicine, as it appeared by many Philosophers' Books. Alchemy therefore is a science teaching how to make and compound a certain medicine, which is called Elixir, the which when it is cast upon metals or imperfect bodies, does fully perfect them in the very projection.

CHAPTER II.
Of the natural principles, and procreation of Minerals.

Secondly, I will perfectly declare the natural principles and procreations of Minerals: where first it is to be noted, that the natural principles in the mines, are Argent-vive, and Sulphur. All metals and minerals, whereof there be sundry and diverse kinds, are begotten of these two: but: I must tell you, that nature always intends and strives to the perfection of Gold: but many accidents coming between, change the metals, as it is evidently to be seen in diverse of the Philosophers books. For according to the purity and impurity of the two aforesaid principles, Argent-vive, and Sulphur, pure, and impure metals are engendered: to wit, Gold, Silver, Steel, Lead, Copper, and Iron: of whose nature, that is to say, purity, and impurity, or unclean superfluity and defect, give ear to that which follows.

Of the nature of Gold.
Gold is a perfect body, engendered of Argent-vive pure, fixed, clear, red, and of Sulphur clean, fixed, red, not burning, and it wants nothing.

Of the nature of silver.
Silver is a body, clean, pure, and almost perfect, begotten of Argent-vive, pure, almost fixed, clear, and white, and of such a like Sulphur: It wants nothing, save a little fixation, color, and weight.

Of the nature of Steel.
Steel is a body clean, imperfect, engendered of Argent-vive pure, fixed & not fixed clear, white outwardly, but red inwardly, and of the like Sulphur. It wants only decoction or digestion,

Of the nature of Lead.
Lead is an unclean and imperfect body, engendered of Argent-vive impure, not fixed, earthy, dressy, somewhat white outwardly, and red inwardly, and of such a Sulphur in part burning, It wants purity, fixation, color, and firing.

Of the nature of Copper.
Copper is an unclean and imperfect body, engendered of Argent-vive, impure, not fixed, earthy, burning, red not clear, and of the like

Sulphur. It wants purity, fixation, and weight: and has too much of an impure color, and earthiness not burning.

Of the nature Iron.

Iron is an unclean and imperfect body, engendered of Argent-vive impure, too much fixed, earthy, burning, white and red not clear, and of the like Sulphur: It wants fusion, purity, and weight: It has too much fixed unclean Sulphur, and burning earthiness. That which has been spoken, every Alchemist must diligently observe.

CHAPTER III.
Out of what things the matter of Elixir must be more nearly extracted.

The generation of metals, as well perfect, as imperfect, is sufficiently declared by that which has been already spoken, Now let us return to the imperfect matter that must be chosen and made perfect. Seeing that by the former Chapters we have been taught, that all metals are engendered of Argent-vive and Sulphur, and how that their impurity and uncleanness does corrupt, and that nothing may be mingled with metals which have not been made or sprung from them, it: remains clean enough, that no strange thing which has not his original from these two, is able to perfect them, or to make a Change and new transmutation of them: so that it is to be wondered at, that any wise man should set his mind upon living creatures, or vegetables which are far off, when there be minerals to be found near enough: neither may we in any way think, that any of the Philosophers placed the Art in the said remote things, except it were by way of comparison: but of the aforesaid two, all metals are made, neither does any thing cleave unto them or is joined with them, not yet changes them, but that which is of them, and so of right we must take Argent-vive and Sulphur for the matter of our stone: Neither does Argent-vive by itself alone, nor Sulphur by itself alone, beget any metal, but of the commixtion of them both, diverse metals and minerals are diversely brought forth. Our matter therefore must be chosen of the commixtion of them both: but our final secret is most excellent, and most hidden, to wit, of what mineral thing that is more near than others, it should be made: and in making choice hereof, we must be very wary. I put the case then, if our matter were first of all drawn out of vegetables, (of which sort are herbs, trees, and whatsoever springs out of the earth) here we must first make Argent-vive & Sulphur, by a long decoction, from which things, and their operation we are excused: for nature herself offers unto us Argent-vive and Sulphur. And if we should draw it from living creatures (of which sort is man's blood, hair, urine, excrements, hens' eggs, and what else proceed from living creatures) we must likewise out of them extract Argent-vive and Sulphur by decoction, from which we are freed, as we were before. Or if we should choose it out of middle minerals (of which sort are all kinds of Magnesia, Marchasites, of Tutia, Coppers, Allums, Baurach, Salts, and many other) we should likewise, as afore, extract Argent-vive and Sulphur by decoction: from which as from the former, we are also excused. And if we should take one of the seven spirits by itself, as Argent-vive, or Sulphur alone, or Argent-vive and one of the two Sulphurs, or Sulphur-vive, or Auripigment, or Citrine Arsenicum, or red alone, or the like: we should never effect it, because since nature does never perfect anything without equal commixtion of both, neither can we: from these therefore, as from the foresaid Argent-vive and Sulphur in their nature we are excused. Finally, if we should choose them, we should mix everything as it is, according to a due proportion, which no man knows, and afterward decoct it to coagulation, into a solid lump: and therefore we are excused from receiving both of them in their proper nature: to wit, Argent-vive and Sulphur, seeing we know not their proportion, and that we may meet with bodies, wherein we shall find the said things proportioned, coagulated and gathered together, after a due manner. Keep this secret more secretly. Gold is a perfect masculine body, without any superfluity or diminution: and if it: should perfect imperfect bodies mingled with it by melting only, it should be Elixir to red. Silver is also a body almost perfect, and feminine, which if it should almost perfect imperfect bodies by his common melting only, it should be Elixir to white which it is not, nor cannot be, because they only are perfect. And if this perfection might be mixed with the imperfect, the imperfect should not be perfected with the perfect, but rather their perfection's should be diminished by the imperfect, and become imperfect. But if they were more than perfect, either in a two-fold, four-fold, hundred-fold, or larger proportion, they might then well perfect the imperfect. And forasmuch as nature does always work simply, the perfection which is in them is simple, inseparable, and incommiscible, neither may they by art be put in the stone, for ferment to shorten the work, and so brought to their former state, because the most volatile does overcome the most fixed. And for that gold is a perfect body, consisting of Argent-vive, red and clear, and of such a Sulphur, therefore we choose it not for the matter of our stone to the red Elixir, because it is so simply perfect, without artificial mundification, and so strongly digested and fed with a natural heat, that with our artificial fire, we are scarcely able to work on gold or silver, And though nature does perfect anything, yet she cannot thoroughly mundify, or perfect and purify it, because she simply works on that which she has. If therefore we should choose gold or silver for the matter of the stone, we should hard and scantly find fire working in them. And although we are not ignorant of the fire, yet could we not come to the thorough mundification and perfection of it, by reason of his most firm knitting together, and natural composition: we are therefore excused for taking the first too red, or the second too white, seeing we may find out a thing or some body of as clean, or rather more clean Sulphur and Argent-vive, on which nature has wrought little or nothing at all, which with our artificial fire, and experience of our art, we are able to bring unto his due concoction, mundification, color and fixation, continuing our ingenious labor upon it. There must therefore be such a matter chosen, where in there is Argent-vive, clean, pure, clear, white and red, not fully complete, but equally and proportionably commixt after a due manner with the like Sulphur, and congealed into a solid mass, that by our wisdom and discretion, and by our artificial fire, we may attain unto the uttermost cleanness of it, and the purity of the same, and bring it to that pass, that after the work ended, it might be a thousand thousand times more strong and perfect, then the simple bodies themselves, decoct by their natural heat. Be therefore wise: for if you shall be subtle and witty in my Chapters (wherein by manifest prose I have laid open the matter of the stone easy to be known) you shall taste of that delightful thing, wherein the whole intention of the Philosophers is placed.

CHAPTER IIII.
Of the manner of working, and of moderating, and continuing the fire.

I hope ere this time you have already found out by the words already spoken (if you are not most dull, ignorant, and foolish) the certain matter of the learned Philosophers blessed stone, whereon Alchemy works, while we endeavor to perfect the imperfect, and that with things more then perfect. And for that nature has delivered us the imperfect only with the perfect, it is our part to make the matter (in the former Chapters declared unto us) more then perfect by our artificial labor. And if we know not the manner of working, what is the cause that we do not see how nature (which of long time has perfected metals) does continually work! Do we not see, that in the Mines through the continual heat that is in the mountains thereof, the grossness of water is so decocted and thickened, that in continuance of time it becomes Argent-vive? And that of the fatness of the earth through the same heat and decoction, Sulphur is engendered! And that through the same heat without intermission continued in them, all metals are engendered of them according to their purity and impurity? and that nature does by decoction alone perfect or make all metals, as well perfect as imperfect? 0 extreme madness! what, I pray you, constrains you to seek to perfect the foresaid things by strange melancholical and fantastical regiments! as one says: Woe to you that will overcome nature, and make metals more then perfect by a new regiment, or work sprung from your own senseless brains. God has given to nature a straight way, to wit, continual concoction, and you like fools despise it, or else know it not. Again, fire and Azot, are sufficient for you. And in another place, Heat perfects all things. And elsewhere, see, see, see, and be not weary. And in another place, let your fire be gentle, and easy, which being always equal, may continue burning: and let it not increase, for if it does, you shall suffer great loss. And in another place, Know you that in one thing, to wit, the stone, by one way, to wit, decoction, and in one vessel the whole mastery is performed. And in another place, patiently, and continually, and in another place, grind it seven times. And in another place, It is ground with fire, And in another place, this work is very like to the creation of man: for as the Infant in the beginning is nourished with light meats, but the bones being strengthened with stronger: so this mastery also, first it must have an easy fire, whereby we must always work in every essence of decoction. And though we always speak of a gentle fire, yet in truth, we think that in governing the work, the fire must always by little and little be increased and augmented unto the end.

CHAPTER V.
Of the quality of the Vessel and Furnace.

The means and manner of working, we have already determined: now we are to speak of the Vessel and Furnace, in what sort, and of what things they must be made. Whereas nature by a natural fire decocts the metals in the Mines, she denies the like decoction to be made without a vessel fit for it. And if we propose to imitate nature in concocting, wherefore do we reject her vessel! Let us first of all therefore, see in what place the generation of metals is made. It does evidently appear in the places of Minerals, that in the bottom of the mountain there is heat continually alike, the nature whereof is always to ascend, and in the ascension it always dries up, and coagulates the thicker or grosser water hidden in the belly, or veins of the earth, or mountain, into Argent-vive. And if the mineral fatness of the same place arising out of the earth, be gathered warm together in the veins of the earth, it runs through the mountain, and becomes Sulphur. And as a man may see in the foresaid veins of that place, that Sulphur engendered of the fatness of the earth (as is before touched) meets with the Argent-vive (as it is also written) in the veins of the earth, and begets the thickness of the mineral water. There, through the continual equal heat in the mountain, in long process of time diverse metals are engendered, according to the diversity of the place. And in these Mineral places, you shall find a continual heat. For this cause we are of right to note, that the external mineral mountain is everywhere shut up within itself, and stony: for if the heat might issue out, there should never be engendered any metal. If therefore we intend to immitate nature, we must needs have such a furnace like unto the Mountains, not in greatness, but in continual heat, so that the fire put in, when it ascends, may find no vent: but that the heat may beat upon the vessel being close shut, containing in it the matter of the stone: which vessel must be round, with a small neck, made of glass or some earth, representing the nature or close knitting together of glass: the mouth whereof must be signed or sealed with a covering of the same matter, or with lute. And as in the mines, the heat does not immediately touch the matter of Sulphur and Argent-vive, because the earth of the mountain comes everywhere between: So this fire must not immediately touch the vessel, containing the matter of the aforesaid things in it, but it must be put into another vessel, shut closed in the like manner, that so the temperate heat may touch the matter above and beneath, and where ever it be, more aptly and fitly: whereupon Aristotle says, in the light of lights, that Mercury is to be concocted in a three-fold vessel, and that the vessel must be of most hard Glass, or (which is better) of Earth possessing the nature of Glass.

CHAPTER VI.

Of the accidental and essential colours appearing in the work.

The matter of the stone thus ended, you shall know the certain manner of working, by what manner and regiment, the stone is often changed in decoction into diverse colors. Whereupon one says, So many colors, so many names. According to the diverse colors appearing in the work, the names likewise were varied by the Philosophers: whereon, in the first operation of our stone, it is called putrifaction, and our stone is made black: whereof one says, When you find it black, know that in that blackness whiteness is hidden, and you must extract the same from his most subtle blackness. But after putrifaction it waxes red, not with a true redness, of which one says: It is often red, and often of a citrine color, it often melts, and is often coagulated, before true whiteness. And it dissolves itself, it coagulates itself, it putrifies itself, it colors itself, it mortifies itself, it quickens itself it makes itself black, it makes itself white, it makes itself red. It is also green: whereon another says, Concoct it, till it appears green unto you, and that is the soul. And another, Know, that in that: green his soul bears dominion. There appears also before whiteness the peacocks color, whereon one says thus, Know you that all the colors in the world, or that may be imagined, appear before whiteness, and afterward true whiteness follows. Whereof one says: When it has been decocted pure and clean, that it shines like the eyes of fishes, then are we to expect his utility, and by that time the stone is congealed round, And another says: When you shall find whiteness atop in the glass, be assured that in that whiteness, redness is hidden: and this you must extract: but concoct it while it becomes all red: for between true whiteness and true redness, there is a certain ash-color: of which it is said, After whiteness, you cannot err, for increasing the fire, you shall come to an ash-color: of which another says: Do not set light by the ashes, for God shall give it to you molten: and then at the last the King is invested with a red crown the by will of God.

CHAPTER VII.

How to make projection of the medicine upon any imperfect body.

I have largely accomplished my promise of that great mastery, for making the most excellent Elixir, red and white. For conclusion, we are to treat of the manner of projection, which is the accomplishment of the work, the desired and expected joy. The red Elixir turns into a citrine color infinitely, and changes all metals into pure gold. And the white Elixir does infinitely whiten, and brings every metal to perfect whiteness. But we know that one metal is farther off from perfection then another, and one more near then another. And although every metal may by Elixir be reduced to perfection, nevertheless the nearest are more easily, speedily, and perfectly reduced, then those which are far distant, And when we meet with a metal that is near to perfection, we are thereby excused from many that are far off. And as for the metals which of them be near, and which far off, which of them I say be nearest to perfection, if you are wise and discrete, you shall find to be plainly and truly set out in my Chapters. And without doubt, he that is so quick sighted in this my Mirror, that by his own industry he can find out the true matter, he does full well know upon what body the medicine is to be projected to bring it to perfection. For the forerunners of this Art, who have found it out by their philosophy, do point out with their finger the direct and plain way, when they say: Nature, contains nature: Nature overcomes nature: and Nature meeting with her nature, exceedingly rejoices, and is changed into other natures, And in another place, Every like rejoices in his like: for likeness is said to be the cause of friendship, whereof many Philosophers have left a notable secret, Know you that the sour does quickly enter into his body, which may by no means be joined to another body, And in another place, The soul does quickly enter into his own body, which if you go about to join with another body, you shall loose your labor: for the nearness itself is more clear. And because corporeal things in this regiment are made incorporeal, and contrariwise things incorporeal corporeal, and in the shutting up of the work, the whole body is made a spiritual fixed thing: and because also that spiritual Elixir evidently, whether white or red, is so greatly prepared and decocted beyond his nature, it is no marvel that it cannot be mixed with a body, on which it is projected, being only melted. It is also a hard matter to Project it on a thousand thousand and more, and incontinently to penetrate and transmute them. I will therefore now deliver unto you a great and hidden secret. one part is to be mixed with a thousand of the next body, and let: all this be surely put into a fit vessel, and set it in a furnace of fixation, first with a lent fire, and afterwards increasing the fire for three days, till they be inseparably joined together, and this is a work of three days: then again and finally every part hereof by itself, must be projected upon another thousand parts of any near body: and this is a work of one day, Or one hour, or a moment, for which our wonderful God is eternally to be praised.

Here ends the Mirror of Alchemy, composed by the most learned Philosopher, Roger Bacon.

BACON, ROGER. The 13th century, an age peculiarly rich in great men, produced few, if any, who can take higher rank than Roger Bacon. He is in every way worthy to be placed beside such thinkers as Albertus Magnus, Bonaventura, and Thomas Aquinas. These had an infinitely wider renown in their day, while he was ignored by his contemporaries and neglected by his successors; but modern criticism has restored the balance in his favour, and is even in danger of going equally far in the opposite direction. Bacon, it is now said, was not appreciated by his age because he was so completely in advance of it; he is a 16th or 17th century philosopher, whose lot has been by some accident cast in the 13th century; he is no schoolman, but a modern thinker, whose conceptions of science are more just and clear than are even those of his more celebrated namesake.[1] In this view there is certainly a considerable share of truth, but it is much exaggerated. As a general rule, no man can be completely dissevered from his national antecedents and surroundings, and Bacon is not an exception. Those who take up such an extreme position regarding his merits have known too little of the state of contemporary science, and have limited their comparison to the works of the scholastic theologians. We never find in Bacon himself any consciousness of originality; he has no fresh creative thought or method to introduce whereby the face of science may be changed; he is rather a keen and systematic thinker, who is working in a well-beaten track, from which his contemporaries were being drawn by the superior attractions of theology and metaphysics.

Roger Bacon was born in 1214, near Ilchester, in Somersetshire. His family appears to have been in good circumstances, for he speaks of his brother as wealthy, and he himself expended considerable sums on books and instruments; but in the stormy reign of Henry III. they suffered severely, their property was despoiled, and several members of the family were driven into exile. Roger completed his studies at Oxford, though not, as current traditions assert, at Merton or at Brazenose, neither of those colleges having then been founded. His great abilities were speedily recognised by his contemporaries, and he came to be on terms of close intimacy with some of the most independent thinkers of the time. Of these the most prominent were Adam de Marisco and Robert Grosseteste (*Capito*), afterwards bishop of Lincoln, a man of liberal mind and wide attainments, who had especially devoted himself to mathematics and experimental science.

Very little is known of Bacon's life at Oxford; it is said he took orders in 1233, and this is not improbable. In the following year, or perhaps later, he crossed over to France, and studied for a considerable length of time at the university of Paris, then the centre of intellectual life in Europe. The years Bacon spent there were unusually stirring. The two great orders, the Franciscans and Dominicans, were in the vigour of youth, and had already begun to take the lead in theological discussion. Alexander of Hales, the author of the great *Summa*, was the oracle of the Franciscans, while the rival order rejoiced in Albertus Magnus, and in the rising genius of the angelic doctor, Thomas Aquinas.

The scientific training which Bacon had received, partly by instruction, but more from the study of the Arab writers, made patent to his eyes the manifold defects in the imposing systems reared by these doctors. It disgusted him to hear from all around him that philosophy was now at length complete, that it had been reduced into compact order, and was being set forth by a certain professor at Paris. Even the great authority on which they reposed, Aristotle, was known but in part, and that part was rendered well-nigh unintelligible through the vileness of the translations; yet not one of those professors would learn Greek so that they might arrive at a real knowledge of their philosopher. The Scriptures, if read at all in the schools, were read in the erroneous versions; but even these were being deserted for the *Sentences* of Peter Lombard. Physical science, if there was anything deserving that name, was cultivated, not by experiment in the true Aristotelian way, but by discussion and by arguments deduced from premises resting on authority or custom. Everywhere there was a show of knowledge covering and concealing fundamental ignorance. Bacon, accordingly, who knew what true science was, and who had glimpses of a scientific *organon* or method, withdrew from the usual scholastic routine, and devoted himself to languages and experimental researches. Among all the instructors with whom he came in contact in Paris, only one gained his esteem and respect; this was an unknown individual, Petrus de Maharncuria Picardus, or of Picardy, probably identical with a certain mathematician, Petrus Peregrinus of Picardy, who is perhaps the author of a MS. treatise, *De Magnete*, contained in the Bibliothèque Imperiale at Paris. The contrast between the obscurity of such a man and the fame enjoyed by the fluent young doctors of the schools seems to have roused Bacon's indignation. In the *Opus Minus* and *Opus Tertium* he pours forth a violent tirade against Alexander of Hales, and against another professor, not mentioned by name, but spoken of as alive, and blamed even more severely than Alexander. This anonymous writer, he says, who entered the order when young (*puerulus*), who had received no proper or systematic instruction in science or philosophy, for he was the first in his order to teach such subjects, acquired his learning by teaching others, and adopted a dogmatic tone, which has caused him to be received at Paris with applause as the equal of Aristotle, Avicenna, or Averroes. He has corrupted philosophy more than any other; he knows nothing of optics or perspective, and yet has presumed to write *de naturalibus*; he is ignorant of speculative alchemy, which treats of the origin and generation of things; he, indeed, is a man of infinite industry, who has read and observed much, but all his study is wasted because he is ignorant of the true foundation and method of science.[2]

It is probable that Bacon, during his stay in Paris, acquired considerable renown. He took the degree of doctor of theology, and seems to have received from his contemporaries the complimentary title of *doctor mirabilis*. In 1250 he was again at Oxford, and probably about this time, though the exact date cannot be fixed, he entered the Franciscan order. His fame spread very rapidly at Oxford, though it was mingled with suspicions of his dealings in magic and the black arts, and with some doubts of his orthodoxy. About 1257, Bonaventura, general of the order, interdicted his lectures at Oxford, and commanded him to leave that town and place himself under the superintendence of the body at Paris. Here for ten years he remained under constant supervision, suffering great privations, and strictly prohibited from writing anything which might be published. But during the time he had been at Oxford his fame had reached the ears of the Papal legate in England, Guy de Foulques, a man of culture and scientific tastes, who in 1265 was raised to the papal chair as Clement IV. In the following year he wrote to Bacon, who had been already in communication with him, ordering him, notwithstanding any injunctions from his superiors, to write out and send to him a treatise on the sciences which he had already asked of him when papal legate. Bacon, who in despair of being ever able to communicate his results to the world, had neglected to compose anything, and whose previous writings had been mostly scattered tracts, *capitula quædam*, took fresh courage from this command of the Pope. Relying on his powerful protection, he set at naught the many obstacles thrown in his way by the jealousy of his superiors and brother friars, and despite the want of funds, instruments, materials for copying, and skilled copyists, completed in about eighteen months three large treatises, the *Opus Majus*, *Opus Minus*, and *Opus Tertium*, which, with some other tracts, were despatched to the Pope by the hands of one Joannes, a young man trained and educated with great care by Bacon himself.

The composition of such extensive works in so short a time is a marvellous feat. We do not know what opinion Clement formed of them, but before his death he seems to have bestirred himself on Bacon's behalf, for in 1268 the latter was released and permitted to return to Oxford. Here he continued his labours in experimental science, and also in the composition of complete treatises. The works sent to Clement he regarded as mere preliminaries, laying down principles which were afterwards to be applied to the several sciences. The first part of an encyclopædic work probably remains to us in the *Compendium Studii Philosophiæ*, belonging to the year 1271. In this work Bacon makes a vehement attack upon the ignorance and vices of the clergy and monks, and generally upon the insufficiency of the existing studies. In 1278 he underwent the punishment which seems to have then been the natural consequence of outspoken opinions. His books were condemned by Jerome de Ascoli, general of the Franciscans, a gloomy bigot, who afterwards became Pope, and the unfortunate philosopher was thrown into prison, where he remained for fourteen years. During this time, it is said, he wrote the small tract *De Retardandis Senectutis Accidentibus*, but this is merely a tradition. In 1292, as appears from what is probably his latest composition, the *Compendium Studii Theologiæ*, he was again at liberty. The exact time of his death cannot be determined; 1294 is probably as accurate a date as can be fixed upon.

{{indent| *Bacon's Works.*—Leland has said that it is easier to collect the leaves of the Sibyl than the titles of the works written by Roger Bacon; and though the labour has been somewhat lightened by the publications of Brewer and Charles, referred to below, it is no easy matter even now to form an accurate idea of his actual productions. His writings, so far as known to us, may be divided into two classes, those yet in manuscript and those printed. An enormous number of MSS. are known to exist in British and French libraries, and probably all have not yet been discovered. Many are transcripts of works or portions of works already published, and therefore require no notice. Of the others, several are of first-rate value for the comprehension of Bacon's philosophy, and, though extracts from them have been given by Charles, it is clear that till they have found an editor, no representation of his philosophy can be complete.[3]

The works hitherto printed (neglecting reprints) are the following:—(1.) *Speculum Alchimiæ*, 1541—translated into English, 1597; (2.) *De Mirabili Potestate Artis et Naturæ*, 1542—English translation, 1659; (3.) *Libellus de Retardandis Senectutis Accidentibus*, 1590—translated as the "Cure of Old Age," 1683; (4.) *Sanioris Medicinæ Magistri D. Rogeri Baconis Anglici de Arte Chymiæ Scripta*, 1603—a collection of small tracts containing *Excerpta de Libra Avicennæ de Anima, Breve Breviarium, Verbum Abbreviatum',*[4] *Secretum Secretorum, Tractatus Trium Verborum, and Speculum Secretorum*; (5.) *Perspectiva*, 1614, which is the fifth part of the *Opus Majus*; (6.) *Specula Mathematica*, which is the fourth part of the same; (7.) *Opus Majus ad Clementem IV.*, edited by Jebb, 1733; (8.) *Opera hactenus Inedita*, by J. S. Brewer, 1859, containing the *Opus Tertium, Opus Minus, Compendium Studii Philosophæ*, and the *De Secretis Operibus Naturæ*.

How these works stand related to one another can only be determined by internal evidence, and this is a somewhat hazardous method. The smaller works, which are chiefly on alchemy, are unimportant, and the dates of their composition cannot be ascertained. It is known that before the *Opus Majus* Bacon had already written some tracts, among which an unpublished work, *Computus Naturalium*, on chronology, belongs probably to the year 1263; while, if the dedication of the *De Secretis Operibus* be authentic, that short treatise must have been composed before 1249.

It is, however, with the *Opus Majus* that Bacon's real activity begins. That great work, which has been called by Whewell at once the Encyclopædia and the Organum of the 13th century, requires a much fuller notice than can here be given. As published by Jebb it consists of six parts; there should, however, be a seventh, *De Morali Philosophia*, frequently referred to in the *Opus Tertium*. Part I. (pp. 1-22), which is sometimes designated *De Utilitate Scientiarum*, treats of the four *offendicula*, or causes of error. These are, authority, custom, the opinion of the unskilled many, and the concealment of real ignorance with show or pretence of knowledge. The last error is the most dangerous, and is, in a sense, the cause of all the others. The *offendicula* have sometimes been looked upon as an anticipation of the more celebrated doctrine of *Idola;* the two classifications, however, have little in common. In the summary of this part, contained in the *Opus Tertium*, Bacon shows very clearly his perception of the unity of science, and the necessity of an encyclopædical treatment. "Nam omnes scientiæ sunt annexæ, et mutuis se fovent auxiliis, sicut partes ejusdem totius, quarum quælibet opus suum peragit, non solum propter se, sed pro aliis." (*Op. Ined.*, p. 18.)

Part II. (pp. 23-43) treats of the relation between philosophy and theology. All true wisdom is contained in the Scriptures, at least implicitly; and the true end of philosophy is to rise from the imperfect knowledge of created things to a knowledge of the Creator. Ancient philosophers, who had not the Scriptures, received direct illumination from God, and only thus can the brilliant results attained by them be accounted for.

Part III. (pp. 44-57) treats of the utility of grammar, and the necessity of a true linguistic science for the adequate comprehension either of the Scriptures or of books on philosophy. The necessity of accurate acquaintance with any foreign language, and of obtaining good texts, is a subject Bacon is never weary of descanting upon. He lays down very clearly the requisites of a good translator; he should know thoroughly the language he is translating from, the language into which he is translating, and the subject of which the book treats.

Part IV. (57-255) contains an elaborate treatise on mathematics, " the alphabet of philosophy," and on its importance in science and theology. Bacon shows at great length that all the sciences rest ultimately on mathematics, and progress only when their facts can be subsumed under mathematical principles. This singularly fruitful thought he exemplifies and illustrates by showing how geometry is applied to the action of natural bodies, and demonstrating by geometrical figures certain laws of physical forces. He also shows how his method may be used to determine some curious and long-discussed problems, such as the light of the stars, the ebb and flow of the tide, the motion of the balance. He then proceeds to adduce elaborate and sometimes slightly grotesque reasons tending to prove that mathematical knowledge is essential in theology, and closes this section of his work with two comprehensive sketches of geography and astronomy. That on geography is particularly good, and is interesting as having been read by Columbus, who lighted on it in Petrus de Alliaco's *Imago Mundi*, and was strongly influenced by its reasoning.

Part V. (pp. 256-357) treats of perspective. This was the part of his work on which Bacon most prided himself, and in it, we may add, he seems to owe most to the Arab writers Alkindi and Alhazen. The treatise opens with an able sketch of psychology, founded upon, but in some important respects varying from, Aristotle's *De Anima*. The anatomy of the eye is next described; this is done well and evidently at first hand, though the functions of the parts are not given with complete accuracy. Many other points of physiological optics are touched on, in general erroneously. Bacon then discusses very fully vision in a right line, the laws of reflection and refraction, and the construction of mirrors and lenses. In this part of the work, as in the preceding, his reasoning depends essentially upon his peculiar view of natural agents and their activities. His fundamental physical maxims are matter and force; the latter he calls *virtus, species, imago agentis*, and by numberless other names. Change, or any natural phenomenon, is produced by the impression of a virtus or species on matter—the result being the thing known. Physical action is, therefore, impression, or transmission of force in lines, and must accordingly be explained geometrically. This view of nature Bacon considered fundamental, and it lies, indeed, at the root of his whole philosophy. To the short notices of it given in the 4th and 5th parts of the *Opus Majus*, he subjoined two, or perhaps three, extended accounts of it. We possess at least one of these in the tract *De Multiplicatione Specierum*, printed as part of the *Opus Majus* by Jebb (pp. 358-444). We cannot do more than refer to Charles for discussions as to how this theory of nature is connected with the metaphysical problems of force and matter, with the logical doctrine of universals, and in general with Bacon's theory of knowledge.

Part VI. (pp. 445-477) treats of experimental science, "domina omnium scientiarum." There are two methods of knowledge: the one by argument, the other by experience. Mere argument is never sufficient; it may decide a question, but gives no satisfaction or certainty to the mind, which can only be convinced by immediate inspection or intuition. Now this is what experience gives. But experience is of two sorts, external and internal; the first is that usually called experiment, but it can give no complete knowledge even of corporeal things, much less of spiritual. On the other hand, in inner experience the mind is illuminated by the divine truth, and of this supernatural enlightenment there are seven grades.

Experimental science, which in the *Opus Tertium* (p. 46) is distinguished from the speculative sciences and the operative arts in a way that forcibly reminds us of Francis Bacon, is said to have three great *prerogatives* over all other sciences:—(1.) It verifies their conclusions by direct experiment; (2.) It discovers truths which they could never reach; (3.) It investigates the secrets of nature, and opens to us a knowledge of past and future. As an instance of his method, Bacon gives an investigation into the nature and cause of the rainbow, which is really a very fine specimen of inductive research.

The seventh part of the *Opus Majus*, not given in Jebb's edition, is noticed at considerable length in the *Opus Tertium* (cap. xiv.) Extracts from it are given by Charles, (pp. 339-348).

As has been seen, Bacon had no sooner finished this elaborate work than he began to prepare a summary to be sent along with it. Of this summary, or *Opus Minus*, part has come down and is published in Brewer's *Op. Ined.* (313-389), from what appears to be the only MS. The work was intended to contain an abstract of the *Opus Majus*, an account of the principal vices of theology, and treatises on speculative and practical alchemy. At the same time, or immediately after, Bacon began a third work as a preamble to the other two, giving their general scope and aim, but supplementing them in many points. The part of this work, generally called *Opus Tertium*, is printed by Brewer (pp. 1-310), who considers it to be a complete treatise. Charles, however, has given good grounds for supposing that it is merely a preface, and that the work went on to discuss grammar, logic (which Bacon thought of little service, as reasoning was innate), mathematics, general physics, metaphysics, and moral philosophy. He founds his argument mainly on passages in the *Communia Naturalium*, which indeed prove distinctly that it was sent to Clement, and cannot, therefore, form part of the *Compendium*, as Brewer seems to think. It must be confessed, however, that nothing can well be more confusing than the references in Bacon's works, and it seems well-nigh hopeless to attempt a complete arrangement of them until the texts have been collated and carefully printed.

All these large works Bacon appears to have looked on as preliminaries, introductions, leading to a great work which should embrace the principles of all the sciences. This great work, which is perhaps the frequently referred to *Liber Sex Scientiarum*, he began, and a few fragments still indicate its outline. First appears to have come the treatise now called *Compendium Studii Philosophiæ* (Brewer, pp. 393-519), containing an account of the causes of error, and then entering at length upon grammar. After that, apparently, logic was to be treated; then, possibly, mathematics and physics; then speculative alchemy and experimental science. It is, however, very difficult, in the present state of our knowledge of the MSS., to hazard even conjectures as to the contents and nature of this last and most comprehensive work.

Bacon's fame in popular estimation has always rested on his mechanical discoveries. Careful research has shown that very little in this department can with accuracy be ascribed to him. He certainly describes a method of constructing a telescope, but not so as to lead one to conclude that he was in possession of that instrument. Gunpowder, the invention of which has been claimed for him on the ground of a passage in his works, which fairly interpreted at once disposes of any such claim, was already known to the Arabs. Burning-glasses were in common use, and spectacles it does not appear he made, although he was probably acquainted with the principle of their construction. His wonderful predictions (in the *De Secretis*] must be taken *cum grano salis;* and it is not to be forgotten that he believed in astrology, in the doctrine of signatures, and in the philosopher's stone, and *knew* that the circle had been squared.

-

1. See Dühring, Kritische Ges. d. Phil., 192, 249 51.
2. It is difficult to identify this unknown professor. Brewer thinks the reference is to Richard of Cornwall; but the little we know of Richard is not in harmony with what is said here, nor with the terms in which he is elsewhere spoken of by Bacon. Erdmann conjectures Thomas Aquinas, which is extremely improbable, as Thomas was unquestionably not the first of his order to study philosophy. Cousin and Charles think that Albertus Magnus is aimed at, and certainly much of what is said applies with peculiar force to him. But some things do not at all cohere with what is otherwise known of Albert. The unknown is said to have received no regular philosophic training; we know that Albert did. The unknown entered the order when very young; unless the received date of Albert's birth be false, he did not enter till nearly twenty-eight years of age. Albert, too, could not be said with justice to be utterly ignorant of alchemy, and his mechanical inventions are well known. It is worth pointing out that Brewer, in transcribing the passage bearing on this (*Op. Ined.* p. 327), has the words *Fratrum puerulus*, which in his marginal note he interprets as applying to the Franciscan order. In this case, of course, Albert could not be the person referred to, as he was a Dominican. But Charles, in his transcription, entirely omits the important word *Fratrum*. There are other instances in which Brewer and Charles do not agree, *e.g.*, according to Brewer, Bacon speaks of Thomas and Albert as *pueri duorum ordinum;*

according to Charles, he says, *primi duorum ordinum;* a discrepancy not unimportant.

3.   The more important MSS. are: (1.) The extensive work on the fundamental notions of physics, called *Communia Naturalium,* which is found in the Mazarin Library at Paris, in the British Museum, and in the Bodleian and University College Libraries at Oxford; (2.) On the fundamental notions of mathematics, *De Communibus Mathematicæ,* part of which is in the Sloane collection, part in the Bodleian; (3.) *Baconis Physica,* contained among the additional MSS. in the British Museum; (4.) The fragment called *Quinta Pars Compendii Theologiæ, in the Brit. Mus.; (5.) the* Metaphysica, *in the Biblioth. Impér. at Paris; (6.) The* Compendium Studii Theologiæ, in the Brit. Mus.; (7.) The logical fragments, such as the *Summa Dialectices,* in the Bodleian, and the glosses upon Aristotle's physics and metaphysics in the library at Amiens.

4.   At the close of the *Verb. Abbrev.* is a curious note, concluding with the words, "ipse Rogerus fuit distipulus fratris Alltrtil"